Teachers are here to **guide** you.

Teachers are here to **love** you.

Teachers are here to **play** with you.

Teachers are here to **help** you when you are **hurt**.

Teachers are here to keep you **safe**.

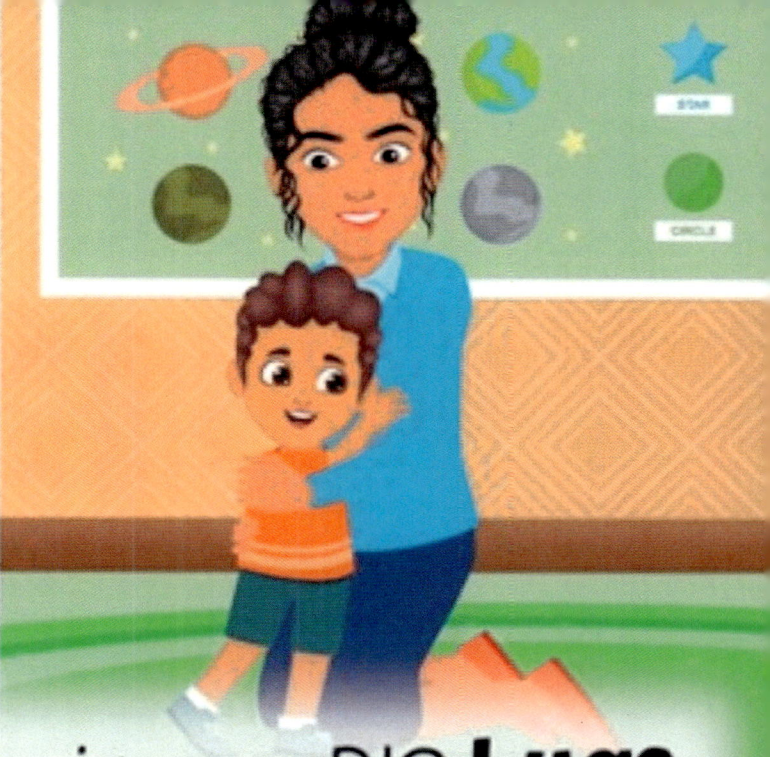

Teachers are here to give you BIG **hugs**.

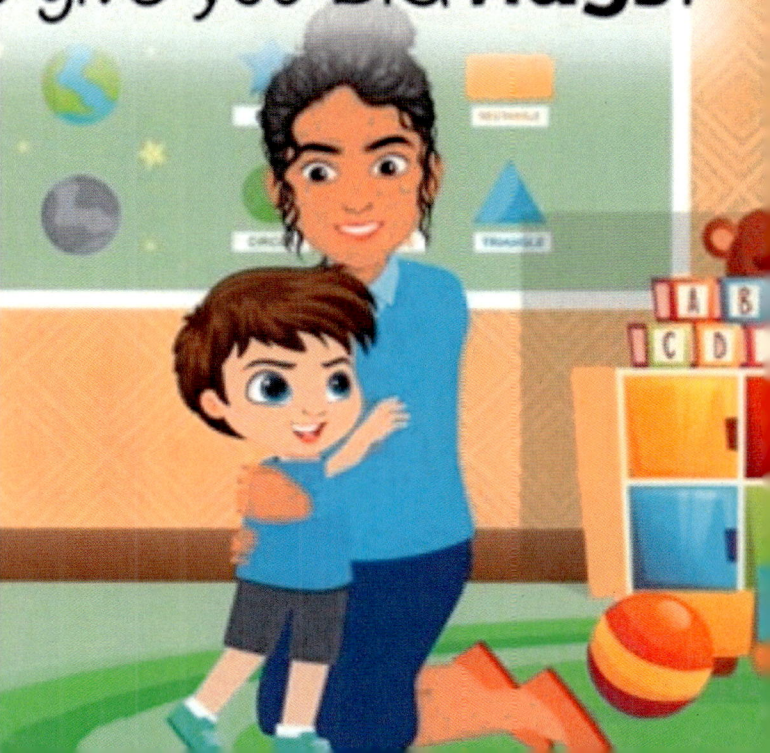

Teachers are here to ensure everyone gets **snacks** during snack time.

Teachers are **superheroes** because they take good **care** of you.

Teachers are very **special** people.

This book is dedicated to the past students we encountered throughout the years. You inspired us to write this book. Check out their incredible artwork.

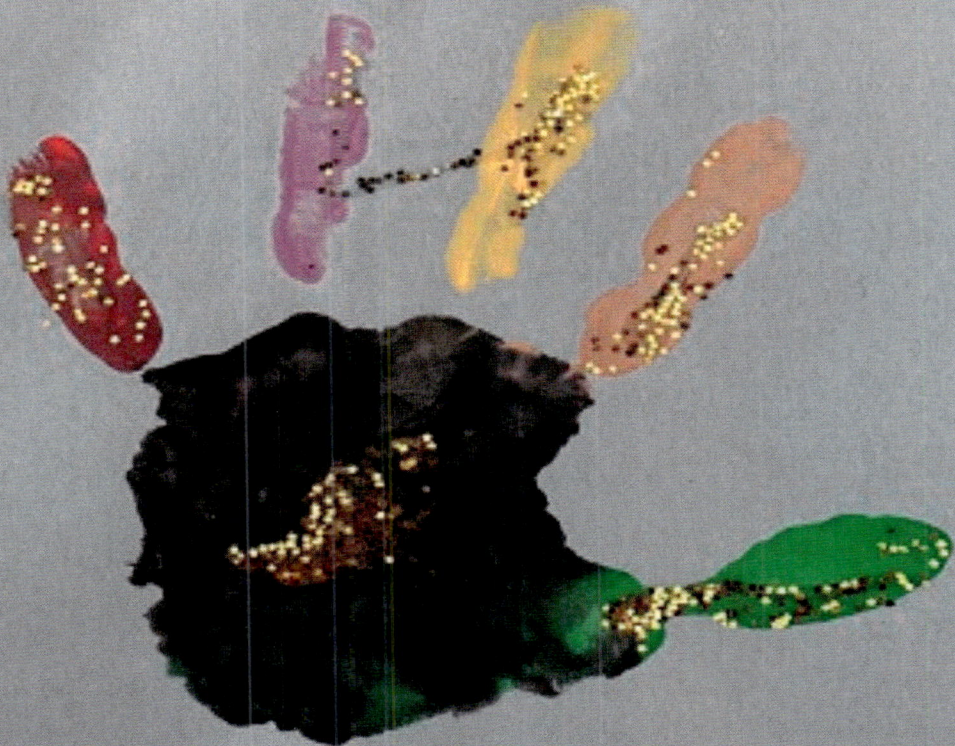

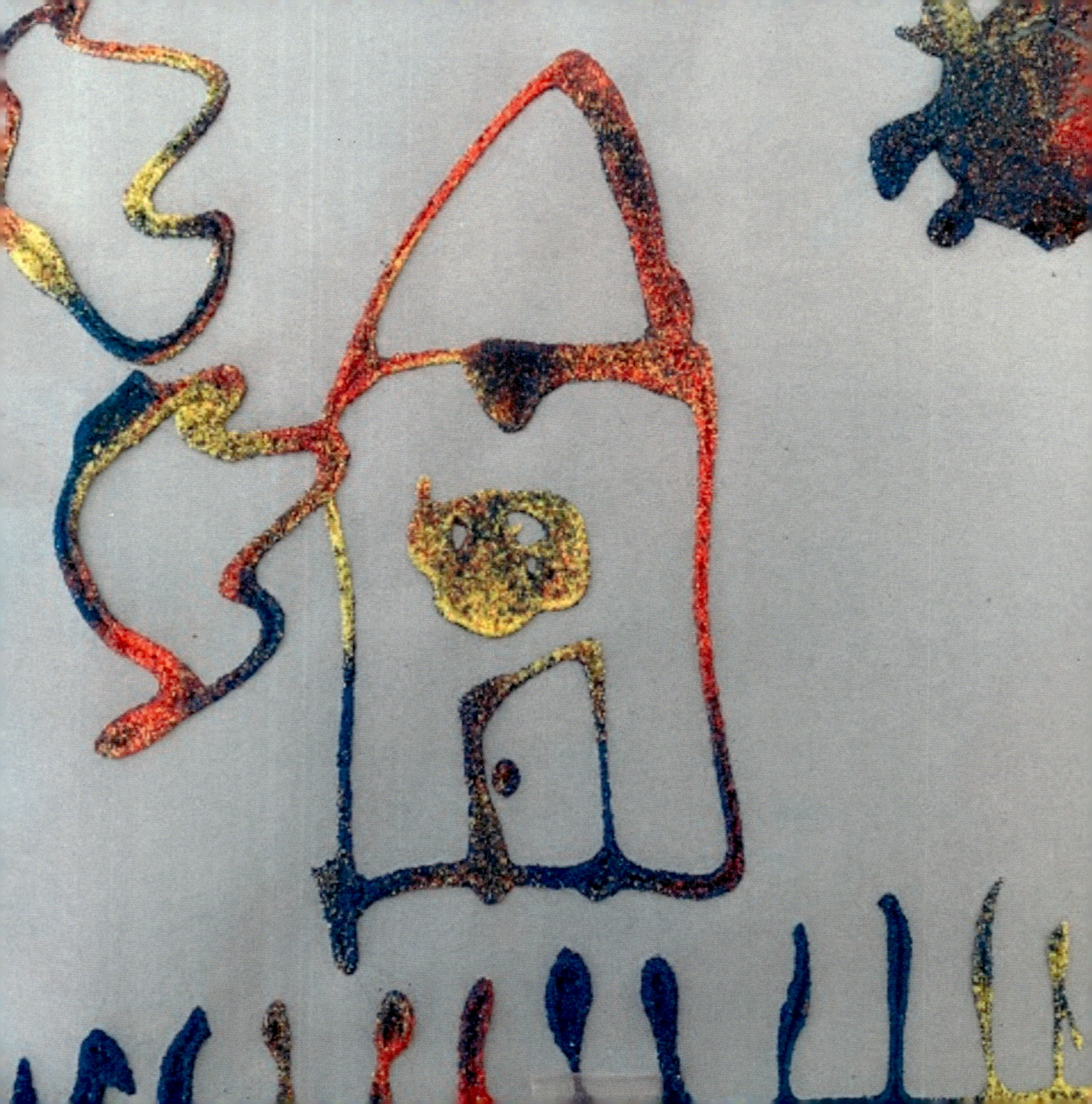

My Dad Rocks!

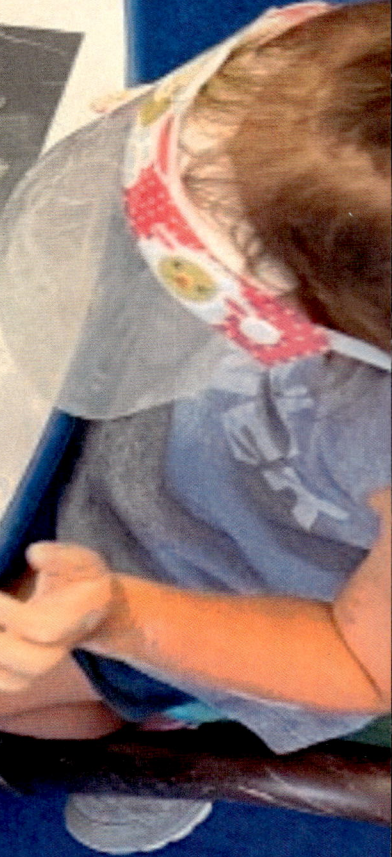

Friendship Tree

Friendship Tree

Brinley

Ms Ariel

Mollie

Our
Friendship
Flower

Kennedy

Thank you!

Teachers

Made in the USA
Las Vegas, NV
29 April 2022